The Civilian Conservation Corps

A Guide to Their Works in Rhode Island

Leo Caisse

Visit our website at www.StillwaterPress.com for more information.

First Stillwater River Publications Edition

Library of Congress Control Number 2019936694

ISBN-13: 978-1-950-33908-2
ISBN-10: 1-950-33908-4

1 2 3 4 5 6 7 8 9 10

Written by Leo Caisse
Photos by Leo Caisse
Additional photos used with the permission of Kevin Klyberg,.from the collection of Al Klyberg

Published by Stillwater River Publications, Pawtucket, RI, USA.

Publisher's Cataloging-In-Publication Data
(Prepared by The Donohue Group, Inc.)

Names: Caisse, Leo, author.
Title: The Civilian Conservation Corps : a guide to their works in Rhode Island / Leo Caisse.
Description: First Stillwater River Publications edition. | Pawtucket, RI, USA : Stillwater River Publications,
    [2019]
Identifiers: ISBN 9781950339082 | ISBN 1950339084
Subjects: LCSH: Conservation projects (Natural resources)--Rhode Island. | Civilian Conservation Corps
    (U.S.)--History. | Rhode Island--History--20th century.
Classification: LCC S932.R4 C35 2019 | DDC 333.7209745--dc23

Dedication

I would like to dedicate this book to the memory of my father Leo Caisse and all the young men who found hope in Franklin Roosevelt's Civilian Conservation Corps in the midst of the depression and who went on to become the Greatest Generation. I would also like to dedicate this book to those teachers who made history so interesting to me: James Gleason at De La Salle Academy in Newport and Professors Walter Mullen and Patrick T. Conley at Providence College.

It is also dedicated to the men and women from the Rhode Island Division of Parks and Recreation and the Department of Environmental Management in whose custody the remnants of the Civilian Conservation Corps are entrusted today.

Acknowledgements

Kathy Marquis and Gary Brown of the Wyoming State Archives; Director Bill Mitchell, Felecia Celeberto, and Robert Henniger of The Rhode Island Department of Environmental Management; Jeff Arnold and Paul St. Pierre, also of the Rhode Island Department of Management who went above and beyond the call of duty showing me CCC artifacts; Catherine Cronk for her tireless online research; Lanham Bundy of the Providence Public Library Reference Department; Douglas Cubbison, President of the Wyoming State Historical Society; Kevin Klyberg for giving me permission to use the notes of his father, Al Klyberg; Christian McBurney, for his research in *The Newport Mercury*; Alan Maul of the Oregon Department of Forestry; Eugene Morris of the National Archives, Records Section; and Cheryl Roffe of the Lane County Museum, Lane County, Oregon.

The stock market crash of 1929 sent America into the throes of the Great Depression. The levels of unemployment and suffering felt by ordinary Americans were unlike anything that had ever happened in the country, including Rhode Island. By 1932, the national unemployment rate rose to an astounding 25 percent. At the time, there was virtually no social safety net to help those without money or food.

Americans looked for a savior in the 1932 presidential race and found one in Franklin D. Roosevelt (FDR), who won the nomination of the Democratic Party. In his acceptance speech at the Democratic National Convention in Chicago, Roosevelt alluded to a program he hoped to implement if elected: a conservation army for young men that would employ them, give them a sense of purpose, and help alleviate the sufferings of their families. Most of the populace forgot about the promise, but after Roosevelt won the presidential election and after only forty-two days after being sworn into office, he ushered through Congress and signed into law the Emergency Conservation Act. This law created the Civilian Conservation Corps (CCC).

Unlike the dark army of Hitler Youth across the Atlantic, Roosevelt created a "Tree Army" from the young men of America. Not only would they learn to work together planting millions of trees, they would promote conservation. With

A collage of activities from Company 1187 located at Howard Hill Road in Foster.

their newfound paychecks, the CCC saved many of these young and their families from starvation. A strong argument can be made that the young men of the CCC would become the foundation for the "Greatest Generation" during World War II.

The first open enrollment for the CCC occurred on April 7, 1933. In Providence at the Federal Building where the recruitment was taking place, there was such an overwhelming turnout that the Providence Police had to be called to restore order. Two weeks later, the first enrollees reported to Fort Adams to begin their orientation. The first two camps opened in Rhode Island were Burlingame and the George Washington/Putnam camps, then Governor Theodore Francis Green got approval for a third camp at Nooseneck Hill Road. To allay union concerns over the program, FDR shrewdly appointed as the CCC national director Robert Fechner, then vice president of the American Federation of Labor, and appointed an advisory council of representatives from the Departments of Agriculture, Labor, and the Interior. Responsibility for operating and building the CCC Camps fell under the jurisdiction of the U.S. Army. Not surprisingly, the CCC would be run on a quasi-military basis. In Rhode Island at the start, the secretary to the Rhode Island Unemployment Relief Commission, ultimately selected Rhode Island enrollees.

To enroll in the CCC, the individual had to be a male U.S. citizen, unmarried, physically fit, and unemployed. Many were selected from families on public relief. In total, some 15,900 Rhode Island young men enrolled with those qualifications. Nationally, a total of about 2.5 million men enrolled in the CCC. As the program matured, the qualifications were modified so that seventeen year-olds could join and the maximum age limit was increased from 26 to 28. Still later, married men were invited to join as well. The program proved to be so popular that FDR, by executive order, enabled 25,000 World War I veterans, and yes, some still needy Spanish-American War veterans, to join regardless of their marital status, but they had their own special camps. Rhode Island had at least one of them. Black men, too, were allowed to enroll, but were housed in segregated camps due to the racial attitude of the time. Unless there were not enough to comprise a whole company, they were mixed in. This happened in Rhode Island.

Rhode Island men were gathered at Fort Adams for training. Later, they were sent to a camp for two weeks at Fort Devens outside Worcester. There they went on hikes, performed calisthenics, played sports, and did some minor manual labor. All the while, Army drill sergeants evaluated each enrollee's ability to work and follow regulations. At the conclusion of those two weeks, the young men received a final physical and inoculations for typhoid, paratyphoid, and smallpox. From there the men were issued a uniform and took the CCC oath.

At first, the young men were housed in tents in camps until they constructed their own barracks. Nationally, there were 4500 camps in the forty-eight states and the U.S territories.

Rhode Island had eight camps, although they were not operated simultaneously or continuously and no more than six at a time. They were (with their official designations):

- P 55 Foster, Providence County
- S 51 Charlestown, Washington County (aka Burlingame)
- S 52, Glocester, Providence County, George Washington Memorial State Forest (aka Camp Putnam)
- S 53, West Greenwich, Nooseneck Hills (aka Stepstone Falls)
- S 54 Hope Valley (aka Arcadia)
- NP 1, Escoheag, Washington County, West Greenwich
- SP 1, later NP 1, Beach Pond State Park, Exeter
- P 56, North Smithfield, Providence County (aka Woonsocket, aka Primrose Black Plain Road)
- Fort Adams in Newport, the U.S. Army headquarters in Rhode Island, also served as the headquarters for the CCC in Rhode Island and in Southeastern Massachusetts (Cape Cod) the 4th District in New England

According to Eugene Morris, National Archives, these were the camps in Rhode Island. There were however some shorter lived camps.

Camp Greene (aka Mount Vernon, aka Foster Camp)

It was known as Company 1187. It was actually located in Foster but named after the closest post office in Greene. This Foster camp only functioned between 1935 and 1937. It was located where the Woody Lowden Recreation Center is today in Foster. The Foster Historical Society has an interesting collection of photographs which depict what a typical camp looked like.

A photo of Camp Greene taken from the entrance.

Primrose (aka Woonsocket Camp)

The Primrose Camp was located in North Smithfield and was originally called the Woonsocket Camp. Camp Primrose, the 1161 company, opened in 1935 on the Cesario Farm near the Primrose train station on the Providence to Pascoag line. It was part of the Providence and Springfield Railroad. The first trail they built was the Black Plain Trail at the entrance of their camp in August 1935. The fire lane known as the Whortle Berry Trail was built in September of that year. The dynamite trail was built so that an explosives shed for demolition could be stored there.

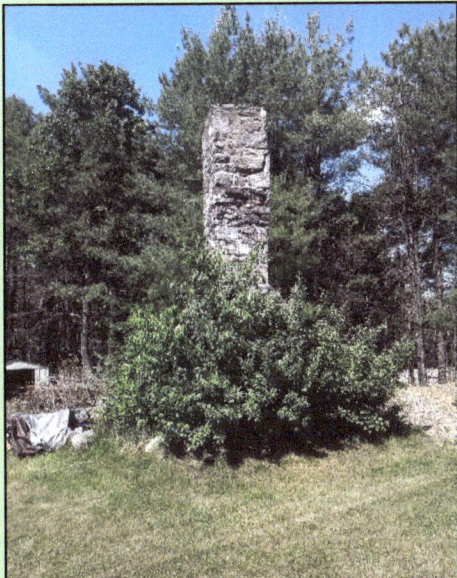

CO. 1161 PRIMROSE – ENROLLEE MEETS FDR

Clockwise from top: A fireplace is all that remains from Camp Primrose in North Smithfield, an article from the Primrose CCC newspaper, and a collage of activities from Co. 1161 Primrose.

They also built the Fire Tower Trail leading to the Woonsocket Fire Tower in February 1937. And they built the fireplaces at Lincoln Woods and the Peter Randall State Park in North Providence. Last but not least, they completed the Diamond Hill Ski Run and toboggan trial in Cumberland at the Diamond Hill State Park in December 1936.

The Primrose Camp was disbanded in 1937 and the men were transferred to the George Washington Camp.

Above: An aerial view of Camp Primrose and some of the men with cows at the camp.
Below: The Diamond Hill Park ski run in Cumberland, a Camp Primrose project, on opening day, January 16, 1938 and today.

Camp Arcadia (aka Hope Valley) Company 1188

In 1935, Rhode Island grew from three camps to six. Camp Kent in West Greenwich was closed, and Arcadia opened, then comprising about 14,000 acres. Today it includes 18,000 acres in the Towns of Hopkinton, Exeter, Richmond and West Greenwich.

Clockwise from top: A water fountain in the woods, a pump house, a working water pump, and another working pump at Arcadia.

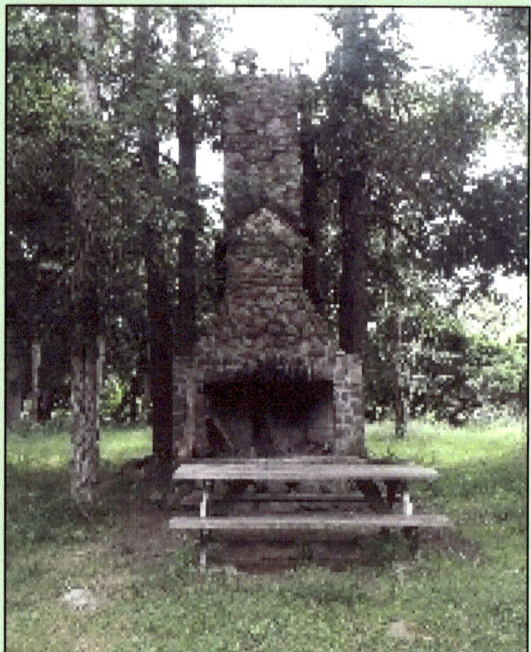

Clockwise from top: A water tower, rediscovered steps in the woods, a remaining chimney, and another water tower.

Clockwise from top: miles of hand-built culverts, one of the many ruins of buildings in Arcadia, a building still in use, a walkway, and another chimney.

The Arcadia group's primary mission was to build fire trails, truck trails, and waterholes for firefighting. The Rockville, Grassy Pond, Tefft Hill, and Sessions Hopkins Trails were cut by this group. About five miles of telephone lines were also installed. Clearing deadfalls and thinning of the forests was performed. Pest management was performed for gypsy moths, and white pine blister rust treatments were undertaken too.

DEM headquarters in Arcadia, a fish hatchery, and a fireplace inside the headquarters.

An aerial view of the camp, and a collage of photos from Co. 1188 Arcadia.

Beach Pond Camp Company 1186

This camp was located where the Rhode Island DEM forestry headquarters is located today, still in its original building. It was laid out by the 141st Company from Burlingame. Many buildings survive until today. They rank from good condition to deplorable condition. They were built by the 1186.

Beach Pond was a park camp whose responsibility it was to build hiking trails along with camping and picnic areas. Their primary mission was forest management.

In 1938, the 1188 Company Arcadia ceased to exist and was replaced by the 1116 V Company from Fort Belvoir in Virginia. No the V didn't signify Virginia, it meant that it was an all veterans unit.

Clockwise from top: The lodge, a pathway at Beach Pond, and a cabin.

One large segment of the unemployed population was veterans that included veterans from the First World War and even some from the Spanish-American War. Before being transferred to Rhode Island, they served in Vermont where they earned the nickname, "The Concrete Company" for their work at the Wrightsville Dam.

In 1940, the 1116V moved yet again, this time to the George Washington State Forest. By that time, the winds of war were on the horizon and CCC companies were being disbanded as the young men were funneled into the armed forces. The veterans' companies, like the 1116V, included men who were either too old to re-enlist or be drafted and were therefore the last to be disbanded. Before their disbandment, one of their last tasks was to cut the Central Trail that connected George Washington with the newly acquired Pulaski Park.

Camp Kent was another camp that was located at the site of what is now the Lineham School in West Greenwich.

Another cabin at Beach Pond.

Clockwise from the top: Another cabin, a large building, a swimming pond and a latrine built by the CCC.

Beach Pond (aka Camp Escoheag) The 1186 Company

This was a park camp administered by the National Park Service, not the forest service. Their specialty was developing tables, shelters, picnic areas, beach facilities, hiking paths, and fire places.

It was originally located on Escoheag Hill in Exeter and later relocated to Lewis City in southwest West Greenwich.

Above: Tercentenary log cabins, located at many entrances to the state, being completed by Co. 1186 at Beach Pond and Escoheag Hill Rd..

An aerial view of the Escoheag camp, and the entrance at Lewis City Road.

Clockwise above: An Adirondack shelter on the Tefft Hill Trail, a counselor's cabin, a cabin for four, and a picnic spot on Breakheart Brook Trail. Below: A collage of photos from Co. 1186.

It began in June 1935 with 23 men to begin building. In July, additional men arrived from Fort Adams to help with the work as well. Soon generators brought electrification to the camp of tents. By October, four buildings were up housing 50 men each along with a mess hall and kitchen. That fall, a camp education program began and they saw the completion of other buildings such as garages and workshops followed by a radio link to Fort Adams and later telephone lines there too. All of this was done while plans were being made to build the Escoheag Fire Tower.

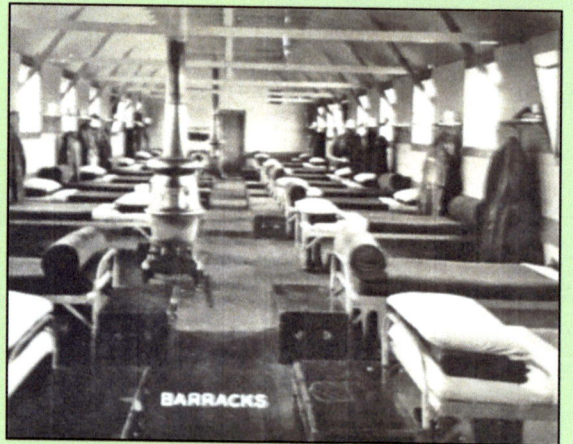

Clockwise: Fort Adams in the 1930's;
and an inside look at a recreation hall, barracks, and mess hall from a typical camp.

As previously mentioned, it was the Beach Pond boys who built the Rhode Island Tercentenary information log cabins.

At Dawley State forest, they built a roadside shelter, outhouse, and 18 fireplaces. It opened in 1937, and was manned by a full-time supervisor who coordinated picnics and overnight camping.

A typical war-time picnic site.

The Lewis City portion of the Beach Pond Camp grew to 53 buildings and was turned over to Rhode Island Camps, Inc. who organized a camp for disadvantaged and troubled urban youngsters. This camp would eventually include lodges for campers and leaders, an administrative building, garage, pump house, and a manmade pond/pool created by a nearby stream which is still there today. Almost all of the buildings were constructed by the Beach Pond CCC. Some of the lodges are still standing but many are dilapidated.

In a report of the CCC work in the last full year of their existence, it was recorded that the Beach Pond builders extended trails at Dawley, built 40 new fireplaces, and constructed four drinking fountains and a sewerage disposal plant.

Alas, all that stands today is a lone chimney and foundation along with some lonesome fireplaces in the forest.

Another area they developed was the LeGrand G. Reynolds Horsemen's Camping area. It included fireplaces, picnic tables, a water pump, a horseshow ring, and riding trails. Interestingly enough, only persons with horses can use it for day use.

All of these accomplishments earned them an award as the best camp in the entire district.

The granite marker at LeGrand G. Reynolds Horsemen's Area.

Camp Putnam
(aka George Washington Memorial Forest)
142nd Company

This camp was established in March 1933. Although it was in Glocester, Rhode Island, it was once again called Camp Putnam because that was the nearest post office in nearby Putnam, Connecticut.

At first housed in tents, they would erect buildings including a mess hall, recreation hall, an education building, wash house, various repair shops, and of course barracks for themselves.

The Putnam boys spent the rest of the year helping to control a gypsy moth infestation along with white pine blister infestations They also started building truck trails and waterholes for firefighting, stringing telephone lines, clearing and thinning forests, surveying boundary lines and planning for a forest fire lookout tower.

A firefighting pool, a waterhole at the camp entrance, a square water pool, and a typical truck trail.

By 1935, Rhode Island had nine fire lookout towers, three of them had been built by the George Washington/Putnam enrollees in 1934. Among them was the George Washington fire lookout tower which was later moved to Escoheag Hill in Exeter.

Clockwise from top: A building still in use, a dynamite shack, inside the dynamite shack, and a collage of activities from Co. 142.

*A CCC memorial, and a fireplace inside one of the buildings
at George Washington Memorial Park.*

Speaking of firefighting, Paul St. Pierre, a long time DEM employee at George Washington State Park, provides all the forestry hose to fire departments throughout Rhode Island.

The GW boys also did work at Goddard Park in East Greenwich. They went on to build a twenty square foot scale model of their camp which was displayed at a sportsmen's conventions from Philadelphia to Boston.

By 1937, they had built 40 miles of truck roads and 200 waterholes for firefighting.

George Washington was closed in December 1937.

Burlingame
(aka Westerly aka Watchaug / aka Charlestown)
141st Company

This camp was the first to be opened in June 1933 with newly minted enrollees from Fort Adams. As they all did, they began as a tent city. During their first year, they built their own wooden barracks, mess hall, administrative and educational buildings, wash rooms, and wood shops. Until federal supplies reached them, they borrowed tools and heavy equipment from the state. They gathered poles from a nearby cedar swamp to start erecting telephone lines for communications and electrical service. They were under the jurisdiction of the National Park Service. They, too, built many truck roads and water holes for forest fire fighting.

A collage of activity photos from Co. 141.

A group photo of Company 141.

In April 1936, the focus of Burlingame changed from a forest camp to a park camp. So from that point forward their mission was beach development, hiking trails, bridle paths, picnic sites, and overnight camping sites for travelers.

They too built the seemingly ever-present open faced Adirondack shelters. A few of the old remnants and fireplaces can still be seen today along the road leading to the Pastore Leisure Center at Burlingame.

The Burlingame boys fielded many championship sports teams and won prizes for displays at the old Kingston State Fair. It was also awarded a prize for being the best camp in the 4th District 1st Corps area which included all of Rhode Island and Cape Cod.

Leo Caisse

An aerial view of Burlingame.

What the Civilian Conservation Corps did here and elsewhere:

Structural Projects
Bridges, fire towers and service buildings.

Transportation Projects
Truck trails, minor roads, hiking trails, airport landing fields, performed erosion control, built check dams, terracing, and planted vegetative covering.

Flood control projects
Included irrigation, drainage, dams, ditching, and channel work.

Forest Cultivation
Included planting millions of trees and shrubs, tree stand improvements, seed collecting and nursery work, forest fire protection and prevention, fire suppression, and insect and disease control.

Landscape and Recreation Projects
Building and fostering picnic and camping areas along with lake and pond site clearing.

Range Improvement
Predator elimination.

Wildlife Projects
Stream improvements, fish stocking, and performed food and cover planting.

Soil Conservation
Promoted the use of contour farming techniques to farmers.

The typical camp started off as a tent city until they eventually built their own structures which included a mess hall, a bath house, officer's quarters, a recreation hall that usually housed the canteen, an infirmary, a library, a garage tool sheds, machine shops and four 50-man barracks building to house on average fifty men each. The CCC enrollees led a structured life with a quasi-military routine. Reveille started the day, after which sleepy men formed for inspection of their barracks after making their beds and cleaning. Then they marched often two by two, in uniform, for their breakfast. Dinner was more formal, held in dress uniforms; black ties were their ticket. After breakfast they would line up for work call. If their work project for the day was nearby they walked to it otherwise they were transported to it via trucks. They would have a morning coffee break and depending how far they were from camp, they would either walk back or have their lunches trucked in to them. They would rest an hour and break for the day at 4 p.m. Dinner time was at 5:30 p.m. Evenings were devoted to whatever they wished to pursue which could be classes, sports, reading, going to town, or vocational education. Lights out was at 10 p.m. and taps was at 10:15 p.m.

Due to their malnutrition, their food portions were five percent higher than those in the regular U.S. Army. The enlistees were sometimes so malnourished that they gained an average of twelve pounds each.

Enlistment was for a period of just six months but enrollees could re-enlist up to a total period of two years, after which they were discharged. After a short absence, a discharged man could start the process all over again, and some did just that.

The pay was good at $30 per month, but the enlistee was required to send $25 of those dollars home to his family. The money sent home saved many families from serious malnutrition and possibly starvation and kept them together. An estimated 12 to 15 million family members were supported in this way.

Being run by the Army during the fascist era of the 1930's could have been a sensitive issue, so there was no drilling, saluting or weapons training. But there was forming into ranks, living in tents (at least until they erected barracks), and sometimes even buglers. Many camps had two movies a week using state of the art movie projectors, chaplain services, lending libraries, sports equipment, and vocational education.

Roosevelt mandated that all the enlistees should be literate. Nationally, an estimated 400,000 illiterate enrollees became readers. A total of 603 different courses were taught in camps nationwide. Among the courses were practical vocational skills such as truck driving, heavy equipment operation, welding typing, carpentry, stone cutting, motor mechanics, radio broadcasting, woodworking, cabinet making, metalcraft and leathercraft. There were also course in social courtesy and first aid.

Camps often had camp newspapers such as Rhode Island's, *Burlingame Beacon,* the *Escoheagan,* and the *Sad Day* at Fort Adams. These afforded opportunities to practice writing and engage in newspaper production. The newspapers often carried cartoons offering aspiring artists an opportunity to practice their skills. The men also composed songs, wrote poetry and put on plays. They fielded baseball, basketball, horse shoe, and soccer teams that played other camps and teams in the surrounding communities. As a matter of fact, Rhode Island's Arcadia camp won the soccer championship in the Southern League in 1936.

The men celebrated holidays in camp, including Mother's Day. In one instance, a commanding officer came around to collect 25 cents from each man to buy a pillowcase to be sent home to his mother as a gift. In another instance, in Rhode Island, according to Boyden-Reynolds, the Rhode Island boys invited their mothers to camp for a dinner and a skit.

The enlistees wore olive drab Army surplus World War I uniforms with black ties. They were given two pairs of shoes (more than some of them ever had) woolen pants, coats, and khaki shirts. If a man was promoted, chevrons were

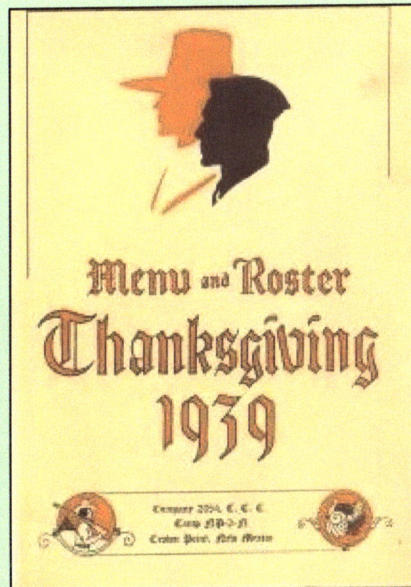

A Mother's Day pillow from the CCC and a Thanksgiving dinner menu.

added to the shirts similar to those of corporals and sergeants in the regular army. Some were selected to serve as leaders in work groups, giving them an opportunity to gain leadership experience.

At the worksite, Army command of the young men was relinquished to another authority. Sometimes it was the park service or other managing body. Locally experience men (LEMs) were frequently put in charge of the work project. The enrollees served as carpenters, stone masons, or whatever the particular job demanded. With the assistance of the LEM's serving as their teachers, they learned new vocational skills, making them more employable upon their discharge. Their typical workday started at 7:15 a.m. and it was lights out at 10 p.m.

In April 1933, the first enrollees began arriving at Fort Adams. By May, 700 young men were in training at the fort and their supervisors praised their morale and enthusiasm. The young men even held a minstrel show with an orchestra, several trios of singers, and the following acts: hillbilly lumberjacks, a clog dancer, a muscular acrobat, a tap dancer, a harmonica trio, musical spoons, and a contortionist.

In May, the first 189 CCC forest men from the 141st Company were sent to the Burlingame Reservation in Charlestown. Soon the 142nd Company was formed and sent to the George Washington Memorial State Forest near Chepachet and were referred to as Camp Putnam after the nearest post office. In June, the 195th Company was sent to Nooseneck Hill in West Greenwich.

Replacements continued to pour in. They were received and inspected for physical examination at the Army's recruiting station at the Federal Building in

Providence and then sent to Fort Adams. Each town had its own quota. For example, Newport had a quota of 28 men, Tiverton 5, Middletown 4, and Jamestown 3.

A handbook and song book for new recruits.

In 1935, it was found that of the 752 recruits received at Fort Adams June 18th and July 15th, 90 had completed high school and of those 6 had attended college, with none graduating. The commentators thought it was impressive that more than half had at least completed the seventh grade. By July 1935, a small group of CCC men had been at Beach Pond in Exeter preparing it for the arrival of the rest of the 1186th Company by building tents with wooden floors until the barracks could be completed. The men traveled in buses as far as Greene in Coventry, and from there CCC trucks conveyed the remaining distance to the camp at the Connecticut/Rhode Island border.

An aerial view of Co. 195, Nooseneck Hill, West Greenwich.

In 1936, the sixteen CCC camps in Rhode Island and southeastern Massachusetts were connected to their headquarters at Fort Adams using short wave radio stations, portable sub stations, and public address systems.

From April 1933 to June 1938, a total of 11,744 Rhode Island men served in CCC camps. Out of this number of 11,121 enrollees, including juniors and veterans, 623 were LEM's, cooks, and stewards. On October 20, 1938, 1655 Rhode Islanders were serving in the CCC, with half working in Rhode Island camps.

Roadside picnic groves The CCC built picnic groves for travelers to rest and eat as they drove to and from the beaches on the southern coast. Some of these groves lasted through the 1960's and the advent of the interstate highway system. The remnants of one still exists on Nooseneck Hill Road. Only the chimney and the foundation of the shelter which once stood there, as well as scattered fireplaces, still remain.

A cabin and pond at a camp for underprivileged children on Beach Pond in Exeter.

Log cabin welcome/visitor centers at some of the state's borders in honor of Rhode Island's 300ᵗʰ anniversary. In 1936, to celebrate the Tercentenary of Rhode Island's founding, the Beach Pond boys constructed log cabins to serve as visitor information booths that were situated at several Rhode Island border locations. They were built at Beach Pond and transported by truck to those places. At the conclusion of the celebration, they were moved to various state parks. They were located at the Old Fall River Road, Route 6, on the East Providence/Seekonk line, in Hopkinton at the junction of Route 3 & 84, Park Avenue in Woonsocket, Route 146, on Foster Center Road Route 6, and in Pawtucket at the state line Route 1A.

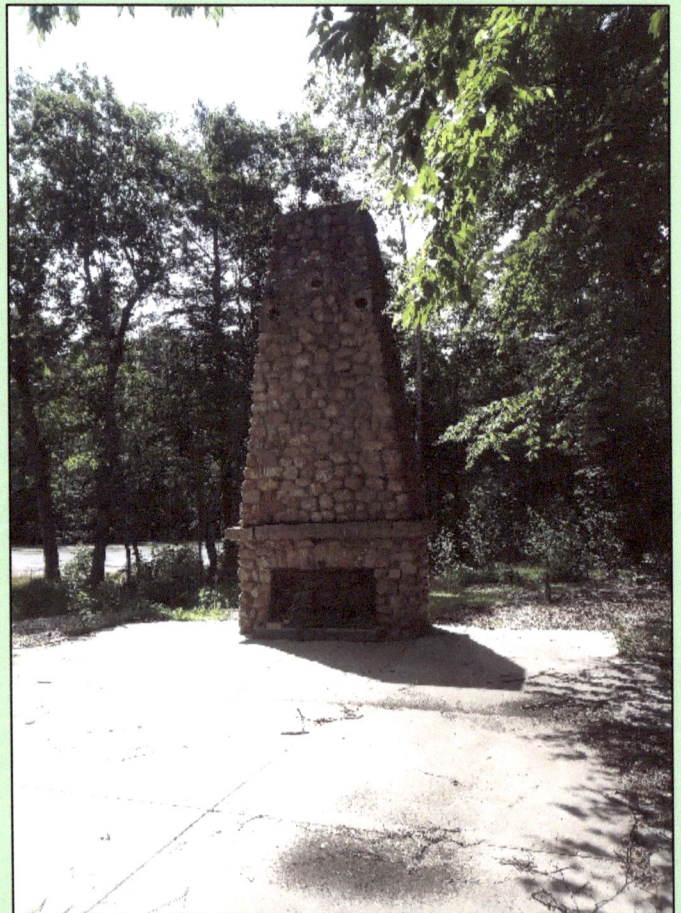

The remnants of a roadside picnic area.

Over 100 miles of truck trails. The trails served as access roads into the forest to aid in forest firefighting; many ended up doubling back trail scenic roads.

Many fireplaces and trails. Works included those at Goddard Park including a building there that still stands serving as the golf club and fireplaces at Lincoln Woods, and a hilltop shelter.

Above: The golf club at Goddard Park.

A fireplace and the remains of a hilltop shelter at Lincoln Woods.

A beachfront at Haines Park on Bullock's Cove in Barrington along with a wooden footbridge which connected Haines to Crescent Park as well as may fireplaces, which, according to local historian Al Klyberg, are considered some of the finest they built in the country. At nearby Squantum Woods, they built in East Providence, they built fireplaces too.

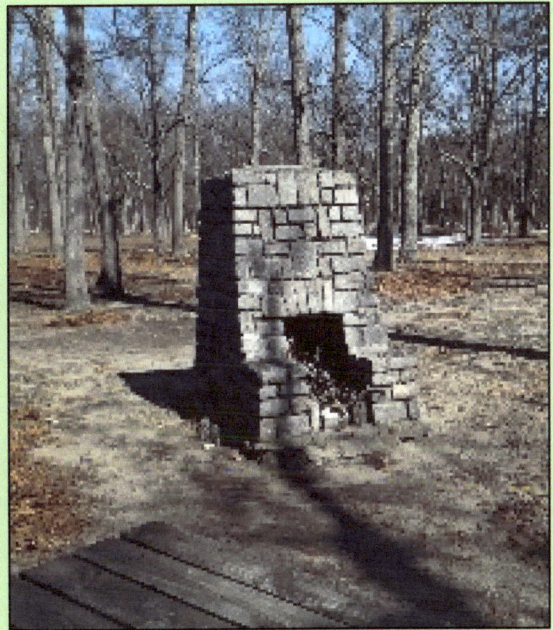

Some of the fireplaces at Haines Park in Barrington.

The footbridge connecting Haines Park to Crescent Park.

The Beachfront at Burlingame State Park includes a beach pavilion which still stands. The remnants of several Adirondack shelters they built there still remain along with fireplaces at the Pastore Leisure Center. They also built parts of Burlingame State Park, Arcadia State Park and Step Stone Falls.

The beachfront pavilion at Burlingame State Park.

Left and above: A fireplace at the Pastore Leisure Center, and the remnants of an Adirondack shelter at Burlingame State Park.

Hiking shelters At least one hiking shelter still stands after having been rebuilt by the Appalachian Mountain Club. It is located in the Arcadia Management Area almost at the intersection of Escoheag Hill Road and Plain Road.

Innumerable wells/ pump houses water fountains, water towers, trailside grills and fire towers. It ought to be noted that these water fountains were built of stone and gravity fed through pipes from a water tower that was in turn fed from a well/pump house.

Right: A shelter rebuilt by the Appalachian club according to the original plans, and the inside of the shelter.

Another hiking shelter.

Occasionally, other federal agencies performed work in the forests. In 1938, for example, under the auspices of the National Park Service, Works Progress Administration workers constructed some buildings at Beach Pond Camp at Escoheag in West Greenwich.

The Hurricane of 1938 not only damaged the coastline but was incredibly destructive of Rhode Island forests. CCC men helped with the cleanup operations and conducted search and rescue and salvage operations. They harvested the fallen timber and even built saw mills to process the lumber and put it into storage areas. This same lumber was used to build military installations in Rhode Island and all over New England when World War II came. It has been estimated that their salvage efforts harvested an estimated 84 million board feet of lumber.

At the Rhode Island State nursery, enrollees helped grow forest tree seedlings. Located on the Pawtuxet River in Cranston, it suffered severe irreparable damage during the hurricane. The CCC undertook the task of salvaging as much as possible and moving it to West Greenwich.

In Exeter, the CCC men built the Voluntown Trail, the Rockville Trail, the Grassy Pond Trail, the Tefft Hill Trail, and the Sessions Hill Trail. The Rockville Trail is one of the best hiking trails in the state.

By 1936, over one hundred miles of one lane dirt truck roads had been cut through Rhode Island forests. While intended initially to assist in forest fire fighting, they had inadvertently created wilderness touring trails. According to a 1935 *Providence Journal* article, weekend motorists out for a spin, hoping for views of babbling brooks and small waterfalls were not disappointed but might expect to run into another automobile coming in the opposite direction. Many trails continue to be used for horseback riding. For example, twenty-five miles of these unpaved roads of yesteryear can still be found along the Putnam Pike near the village of Chepachet in Glocester, Rhode Island, where the CCC had a camp in the George Washington Memorial State Forest.

These back country roads were also in Charlestown around Watchaug Pond at what was to become Burlingame State Park. Roads were also built, and often later became hiking trails in the Wickaboxet State Forest, the Diney Keach Trail, Brandy Brook, Richardson Clearing Trails, the Border Trail crossing into Connecticut and back again into Rhode Island, the Voluntown Trail, the Rockville Trail, Grassy Pond Trail, Tefft Hill Trail, Sessions Hopkins Trail, and Durfee Hill Trail. About 186 miles of trails had been built but only about 100 miles were open to the public. These were unpaved roads that a car or fire truck could travel down. Some had been abandoned town roads which had been upgraded. Other roads were on private land to which the owners had granted the federal and state government's unlimited access. Some private owners gated or otherwise blocked access to the roads. Today, the ones that remain are hiking trails and motor vehicles are not permitted on them. As of 2017, the CCC-built roads, according to the Department of Environmental Management's Division of Parks, still exist and remain open to the public in Pulaski State Park within the George Washington

A picnic shelter and it's interior with fireplace on Wickaboxet Trail.

Management Area in Glocester. The Olney-Keach Trail runs North-South from Jackson Schoolhouse road to Route 44 and the Richardson Trail runs East-West from Olney-Keach to Center Trail. While they are open to the public, they are now very rough and would require four wheel drive vehicles to use them unless on foot or horseback. The road at Burlingame is closed to vehicular traffic.

Another important aspect of the Rhode Island CCC was the work they did in the Pacific Northwest. Short of manpower but not work in that area, the federal government decided to transfer 380 Rhode Island enrollees (two entire companies) to Salem, Oregon and Vancouver, Washington. While most of the conservation work that needed to be done was in the West, most of the unemployed were in the East. A total of 1900 New Englanders were transferred across the country in October 1935.

The selected corpsmen had to secure parental consent if they were under twenty-one. These boys, many from poverty stricken families, began their journey from Fort Adams in Newport. They then boarded in Providence a state of the art special train that included ten Pullman cars, four baggage cars equipped with kitchens, two cars carrying their equipment, and one hospital car staffed with a physician. The baggage/kitchen cars were stocked with enough food and wood for their six day trek. They were led by twenty-six leaders and their assistants. The total cost of the trip per man to the federal government was $133.36. If a man's enlistment expired while in the West, the government provided transportation home.

In Oregon, the Rhode Island boys were primarily involved in building and maintaining roads in privately owned forests. They built fire service guard towers at Walton, Greenleaf, and Alsea. They also built fire lookout towers, trails, and shelters. The CCC 141st Company from Westerly, Rhode Island was absorbed into and became the 2108st Company of the CCC. Its campsite was at Triangle Lake near the Town of Blachly in Lane County in Western Oregon. There they were under the command of the Oregon Department of Forestry working with the West Lane Fire Protection District and also performed tasks for the U.S Forest Service. They also worked on road and trail construction, specifically the

Glenbrook-Horton Road, strung telephone lines, and performed firefighting duties as needed. As a matter of fact, one Rhode Island CCC enrollee was killed by a falling snag while fighting a forest fire.

Another Rhode Island company went on to Washington State in the vicinity of Vancouver. There the CCC's helped to build Deception Pass State Park, the Mt. Constitution observation Tower, the Ginko Petrified State Forest Park, the Mt. Rainier National Park employee housing, the Mt. Baker National Park Ranger Station, the Lewis & Clark State Park, and the Carson National Fish Hatchery.

Here is the story of a Warren, Rhode Island, seventeen year-old who joined the CCC on July 2, 1934. He was assigned to the 141st Company then headquartered at Burlingame in Charlestown. There the teenager learned to drive a truck, earning a license issued by the Department of the Interior. At Burlingame, the teenager and other CCC enrollees engaged in work in both private and state owned forests. They built fire towers, built truck roads for firefighting and logging, strung telephone lines, dug wells, worked on pest control and timber improvement, and built hiking trails, shelters and fireplaces. They helped develop a beach and beachfront pavilion at Watchaug Lake at Burlingame which can still be seen and used today by visitors.

In 1935, the 141st Company and another company from Rhode Island were transferred to Oregon and Washington. The young man travelled there with his

MOTOR VEHICLE OPERATOR'S PERMIT

Left: Leo Caisse at the Burlingame CCC camp.
Above: Leo's driver's license, earned during his time there.
Below: A group photo of Leo's Company 141 at Burlingame.

company to Oregon, where he served the maximum of four consecutive enlistments and was honorably discharged on June 23, 1936. After little more than a year off, the enrollee from Warren re-enlisted in the CCC on September 7, 1937. This time he was sent to the 2130th Company then located near Casper in Wyoming. According to the National Archives historian Eugene Morris, it is difficult to ascertain with any degree of certainty why he was ordered there. Perhaps there was a manpower shortage or a need for a particular set of skills he had learned in the CCC or a personal request. He could now drive a truck, operate a bulldozer, tractor and jackhammer, as well as weld and set explosives for demolition purposes such as removing boulders or removing stumps.

Leo Caisse

He also learned a new skill out there—how to evade mountain lions. The Casper Chamber of Commerce persuaded the National Park Service to send a CCC group there including the 2130th company, to go to the Casper area in 1937. Some of the work performed by the CCC on Casper Mountain included, building bridges, improving roads, and reducing fire hazards. At Fort Casper, they built parking areas, access roads, and a dike in a river, along with forest fire fighting as needed and an occasional coal fire.

Above: A sample of insignia worn on the uniforms of CCC participants.
Below: Leo's discharge papers.

I did not get to know the "teenager from Warren" very well because he passed away unexpectedly at a young age when I was only nine years old. But I still remember being mesmerized although I didn't understand them at the time of his knowing cowboys and Indians. That teenager from Warren was my father Leo Caisse. It has been a great source of pride to learn about his adventures and the environmental legacy he left in Rhode Island and far flung places such as Oregon and Wyoming.

44

By 1940, the dark clouds of war loomed on the horizon. In the United States, the draft began in September of that year absorbing many of the eligible young men. The money allocated to the CCC was re-directed to the War Department. Despite being one of FDR's pet projects and very popular with the public, the CCC was not funded by Congress in 1942, and it came to an end in June of that year. It never was a permanent agency.

The young men from the CCC who were drafted or enlisted in the military took a pay cut. However, the U.S. Army recognized the value of the CCC quasi-military training and frequently promoted CCC veterans to the rank of corporal or sergeant.

Ownership of CCC property often reverted to the War or Navy Departments. Such was the case at Burlingame State Park, where the Navy used the former CCC barracks as overflow housing for pilots training at the nearby Charlestown Naval Auxiliary Air Field.

From time to time, calls to resurrect the CCC have been heard in the public arena. One such bill actually passed Congress in the 1980's but was vetoed by President Reagan.

Unfortunately, few structures built by the CCC remain.

There is a small monument to the Rhode Island CCC, listing seven CCC camps, at the George Washington Management Area ironically in front of one of the few CCC buildings still standing and used.

National Accomplishments of the CCC

- Planted an estimated 2-3 billion trees
- Rehabilitated 800 state parks
- Cleared 52,000 acres for public campgrounds
- Built 125,00 miles of truck roads
- Constructed 46,854 bridges
- Completed 33,087 miles of terracing
- Built 3000 lookout towers, including the famous and still standing observation tower atop 2409 foot Mount Constitution on Orcas Island, Washington
- Strung 89,000 miles of telephone lines
- Carved 13,100 miles of foot trails
- Improved 40,000,000 acres of farm lands through erosion management
- Worked on 32,000 acres of stream and lakebed management
- Revegetated 814,000 acres of rangeland
- Built many of the ski trails at many of the ski resorts in New England
- Contributed to the restoration of Yellowstone National Park, building lodges, garages, and campsites, as well as tackling general environmental projects
- Helped archeologists research prehistoric cultures in the Carolinas
- Built 72 emergency landing fields for airplanes
- Provided 8,000,000 forest fighting days, with some corpsmen paying the ultimate price. Fifteen CCC men lost their lives and thirty eight were injured fighting the Blackwater Creek Fire in 1937. A Rhode Islander enrolled in the CCC's was also killed at an Oregon forest fire when a tree snag struck and killed him. Back in the day, forest fires were fought with picks, shovels and axes – it was back breaking dangerous work. In some areas they fought underground coal fires.

In total, 7,793 men died while serving in the CCC. This was partly due to their youth and inexperience, as well as the relative lack of safety regulations in place at the time, although some did die from natural causes.

Accomplishments of the CCC in Rhode Island

- Roadside picnic groves for travelers to rest and eat as they drove to and from beaches on the southern coast. Some of these roadside groves lasted through the 1960s and the advent of the interstate highway system.
- A camp for underprivileged children on Beach Pond in Exeter.
- Log cabin welcome/visitor centers at some of the state's borders in honor of Rhode Island's 300th anniversary.
- Over one hundred miles of truck trails to serve as access roads into the forest to aid in firefighting; many ended up doubling as back-trail scenic roads.
- Many fireplaces and trails, including in Goddard Park and Lincoln Woods.
- Beachfront (including fireplaces) on Bullock's Cove in Haines Park in Barrington.
- Beachfront at Burlingame State Park, including the beach pavilion.
- Parts of Burlingame State Park, including the beach pavilion.
- Parts of Burlingame State Park, Arcadia, Dawley State Park, and Stepstone Falls.
- Hiking shelters, at least one of which is still standing today after being rebuilt. It is located in the Arcadia Management Area almost at the intersection of Escoheag Hill Road and Plain Road.
- Innumerable wells/pump houses, water fountains, trailside grills, and fire towers.

Occasionally, other federal agencies performed work in the forests. In 1938, for example, under the auspices of the National Park Service.

The Oath

Not all enrollees in the CCC were willing participants. In larger cities, young men were often urged to join by their local precinct police captains as an alternative to the state reformatory. For some, this didn't prove to be the life for them and they later went AWOL. Most, however enrolled voluntarily through the local welfare board which would certify that they met the minimum requirements then they would go through the Army recruiting process already alluded to, only then were they issued a uniform and invited to take the oath.

> *I,* name*, do solemnly swear that the information given above as to my status is correct. I agree to remain in the Civilian Conservation Corps for the period terminating at the discretion of the United States between dates, unless sooner released by proper authority, and that I will obey those in authority and observe all the rules and regulations thereof to the best of my ability and will accept such allowances as may be provided pursuant to law and regulations promulgated pursuant thereto. I understand and agree that any injury received or disease contracted by me while a member of the Civilian Conservation Corps cannot be made the basis of any claim against the government , except as I may be entitled under the Act of September 7, 1916, and that I shall not be entitled, and I shall not be entitled to any allowance upon release from camp, except transportation in kind to the place at which I was accepted for enrollment. I understand further that any articles issued to me by the United States government for use while a member of the Civilian Conservation Corps are and remain, property of the United States Government and that willful destruction, loss, sale or disposal of such property renders me financially responsible for the cost thereof and liable to trial in civil courts. I understand further that any infraction of the rules or regulations of the Civilian Conservation Corps renders me liable to expulsion therefrom. So help me God.*

Their national motto was: *We Can Take It.*

Some Famous Alumni of the Civilian Conservation Corps

- Chuck Yeager, test pilot, first man to fly supersonic
- Robert Mitchum, actor
- Walter Matthau, actor
- Raymond Burr, actor
- Stan Musial, baseball player
- Archie Moore, heavy weight boxing champion
- Hubert D. Humphrey, historian
- Borden Deal, writer
- Stanley Makowski, Mayor of Buffalo
- Henry Gurke, Medal of Honor recipient
- Edward Reybal, member of Congress
- Sgt. Strunk and Ira Hayes, two of the Iwo Jima flag raisers
- Norman Borlaug, Nobel Prize winner. It is said that through his work more lives were saved than anyone in history.
- One out of six World War II veterans served in the Civilian Conservation Corps before Pearl Harbor.

From left to right: Chuck Yeager, Robert Mitchum, Stan Musial, and Ira Hayes.

The She-She-She Camps

Not to be outdone, here is the short story of the She-She-She's, the female counterpart to the CCC.

First Lady Eleanor Roosevelt lobbied to form the She-She-She for young unemployed women and got one, albeit short lived. It did not have the support of FDR or was anywhere near as successful as the Civilian Conservation Corps for young men. They began in 1933, and was under the jurisdiction of the National Youth Administration. All told, there were about 90 camps and served about 5000 young women. The first and biggest camp was called Camp TERA which was an acronym for Temporary Emergency Relief Assistance. The She-She-She program was shut down on October 1, 1937 because it was deemed too costly.

A photo from a gathering at a She-She-She camp.

Who Built the Hannah Robinson Tower?

Virtually all online sources about the land-mark Hannah Robin-son Tower in South Kingstown say it was built by the CCC. However, several local sources claim that the Rhode Island State Department of Public Works (DPW) built it. (There was even an ar-ticle in *The Providence Journal* that reported this.) A representative from the South County Historical Society told me that it was built by the CCC under the di-rection of the state DPW. But according to the records of the state DPW, they did the landscaping but there is no record of them building it. Finally, I spoke with someone at the state DEM and he remembers his father telling him he was a member of the CCC crew that built it.

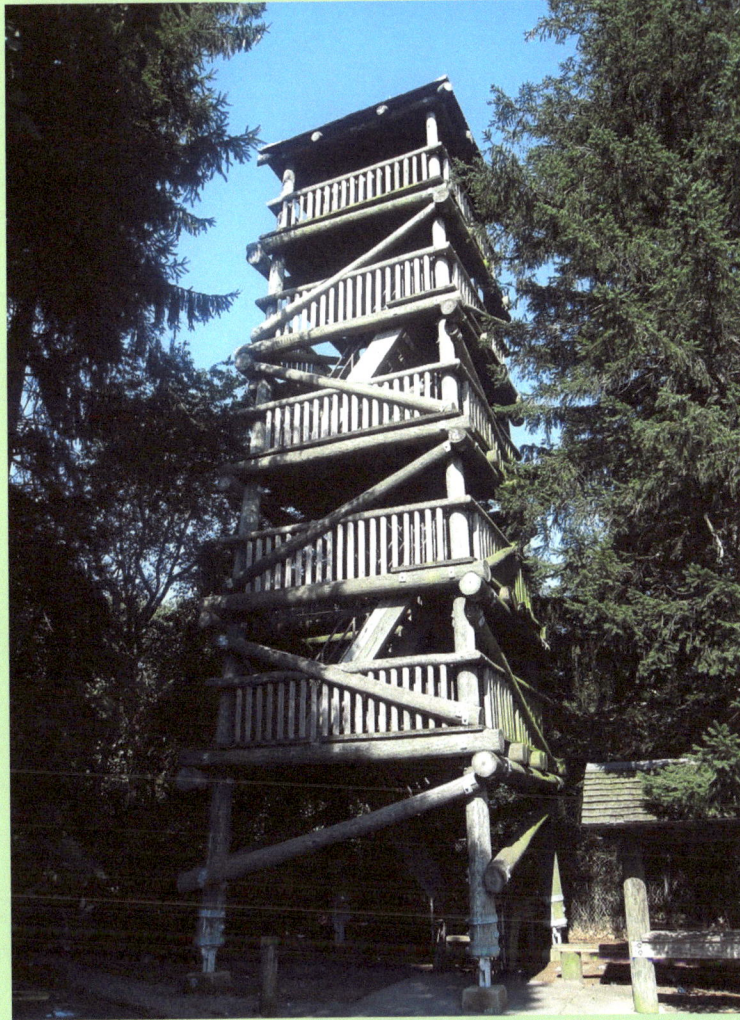

The Hannah Robinson Tower in South Kingstown.

Books

The CCC spawned several books for young people about their adventures while enrolled. Among them were:

Terror in the Tetons, Larry Ahlman 2005
Hitch, Jeanette Ingold, 2006
Big Shoulders, William Jamerson, 2007
Fires in the Wilderness, Jeffrey Schatzer, 2008
Tree Soldier: A Novel of Love, Forgiveness, and the Great Depression, J.L. Oakley
Invasion on the Mountain, Judith Edwards, 2011
Trouble on the Mountain, Judith Edwards, 2012
At the Top of the Mountain, Judith Edwards, 2013

A List of CCC Museums you may want to visit

Colossal Cave Mountain Park, Vail, Arizona

CCC Museum at Camp San Luis Obispo, California

CCC Museum and Memorial, Mount Sano State Park, Huntsville, Alabama

CCC Legacy, Edinburg, Virginia

CCC Museum, Rhinelander, Wisconsin

Florida CCC Museum, Highland Hannah State Park, Sebring, Florida

CCC Museum, Desoto State Park, Fort Payne, Alabama

CCC Museum Waimea, Kauai City, Hawaii

Iowa CCC Museum, Backlore State Park, Strawberry Point, Iowa

CCC Museum, Lake Greenwood State Recreation Area, Ninety-six, South Carolina

Lou and Helen Adams CCC Museum, Parker Dam State Park, Hunter Township,
    Clearfield County, Pennsylvania

Marker Museum at promised Land State Park, Greentown Pennsylvania

New England States CCC Museum, Camp Connor, Stafford, Connecticut

CCC Museum at Pocahontas State Park, Chesterfield, Virginia

New York State Museum, Gilbert Lake State Park, New Laurens, New York

West Virginia CCC Museum, Harrison County, West Virginia

March CCC Museum, Roscommon, Maryland

CCC Museum, Guernsey State Park, Wyoming

Bear Brook State Park CCC Museum, Allenstown, New Hampshire

James F. Justin Museum, online only

Bibliography

Boden, Gary, Reynolds-Booth, Sheila. *The Civilian Conservation Corps in Exeter.* http://www.yorkerhill.com/eha/Stories/Civilian_Conservation_Corps_in_Exeter_RI.pdf

Cohen, Stan. 1984. *The Tree Army: A Pictorial History of the Civilian Conservation Corps 1933-1942.*

Hartt, John. 2013. *Two Hands and a Shovel.*

Klyberg, A. 2009. *100 Years of Rhode Island Parks.*

Lansing, William. 2014. *Camps and Calluses.*

McGrath, Jane. *How the Civilian Conservation Corps Worked.* https://money.howstuffworks.com/economics/volunteer/organizations/civilian-conservation-corp.htm https://money.howstuffworks.com/economics/volunteer/organizations/civilian-conservation-corp.htm

The Newport Mercury, miscellaneous articles - April 28, 1933, p2.; May 19, 1933, p.7; May 26, 1933, p.1.; June 16, 1933, p.2.; June 20, 1933, p.5.; July 27, 1933, p.7; September 28, 1934, p. 4; July 19, 1935, p.2.; November 4, 1938, p.1. and March 29, 1940, p.9.

Moon, Philip Rodman. *The Art of Manliness: The Civilian Conservation Corps Training a Generation in Manliness.* https://www.artofmanliness.com/articles/the-civilian-conservation-corps-training-a-generation-in-manliness/

100 Miles of Trails Built as Aid to Firefighting. August 1, 1935, p.3. *The Providence Journal.*

Rhode Island Division of Parks and Recreation. http://riparks.com/http://riparks.com/

Rhode Island Secretary of State. https://catalog.sos.ri.gov/?p=collections/controlcard&id=2887

Ten Car Pullman Train Starts West. October 26, 1935, p.3. *The Providence Journal.*

Two Forestry Units to go to Camps in Oregon and Washington. October
    24, 1935, p.1. *The Providence Journal,*

United States Department of Agriculture, U.S. Forest Service, Northeastern
    Research Station, in cooperation with the Rhode Island Department of
    Environmental Management, Division of Forest Environment 1998. *The
    Forests of Rhode Island.* http://www.dem.ri.gov/programs/bnatres/for-
    est/pdf/riforest.pdf

About the Author

Leo Caisse, an independent historian, graduated from Providence College with a BA and MA in American History. He has published three articles on the Civilian Conservation Corps having researched his father's service with them. Other historical articles he has had published have appeared in the *East Providence Historical Society Gazette, The East Providence Post, The Barrington Times, The Pawtucket Times, The Valley Breeze, America's World War II Magazine, Small State, Big History*, online and *The New England Historical Society*, online.

www.ingramcontent.com/pod-product-compliance
Lightning Source LLC
Chambersburg PA
CBHW042005100426
42736CB00038B/51